From THE LITTLE MERMAID

ISBN 0-7935-0422-8

Cover art © The Walt Disney Company

Hal Leonard Publishing Corporation
7777 West Bluemound Road   P.O. Box 13819   Milwaukee, Wisconsin 53213

Copyright © 1991 by HAL LEONARD PUBLISHING CORPORATION
International Copyright Secured   All Rights Reserved

ARISE

Words and Music by
MICHAEL COOPER

4

HOT, HOT, HOT

Words and Music by
ALPHONSUS CASSELL

Moderate Latin Dance

O - lé, o - lé, o - lé, o - lé. O - lé, o - lé, o -

lé, o - lé.

F   B♭   C   B♭/C   F   B♭

THREE LITTLE BIRDS

Words and Music by
BOB MARLEY

YOU CAN GET IT IF YOU REALLY WANT

Words and Music by
JIMMY CLIFF

MUSIC SWEET

Words and Music by
WINSTON BAILEY

Pranc-ing in a par-ty, __ in-no-cent
Tell me Mis-ter No-ah, __ tell me when

UNDER THE SEA
(From Walt Disney's "THE LITTLE MERMAID")

Lyrics by HOWARD ASHMAN
Music by ALAN MENKEN

DANCING MOOD

Words and Music by
ALPHONSUS CASSELL

(Spoken:) Look,

we're dancing!

DANCE THE DAY AWAY

Words and Music by DON MIZELL
and LEONARD JONES

44

DAY-O
(THE BANANA BOAT SONG)

Words and Music by IRVING BURGIE
and WILLIAM ATTAWAY

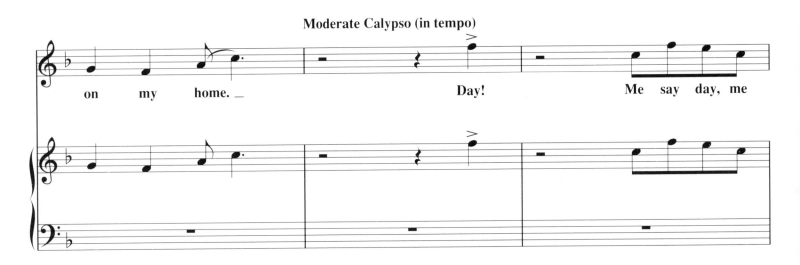

48

TAKE THIS SONG

Words and Music by WILLIAM CLARKE,
MICHAEL COOPER, STEPHEN COORE, RICHARD DALEY,
KENNY GAMBLE, CLAUDINE NESBETH and WILLIAM STEWART

JAMAICA FAREWELL

Words and Music by
IRVING BURGIE

Arise

Words and Music by Michael Cooper

CHORUS
Arise, arise
Wake up and face the morning sun
Let the sunlight open your eyes
Got to realize your time has come
To arise
(Repeat)

In the morning
Everything arise in the morning
Got to realize in the morning
Got to realize it's a new day

And when the shadows moving in the night
Fade away with the morning light
And when the shadows moving in the night
Fade away with the morning light
You'll...

CHORUS (Repeat)

(Repeat first verse)

The fisherman say when the sea get rough
He say, when the going gets tough
You got to show your stuff
You know, it really don't bluff to...

CHORUS (Repeat)

(Repeat first and second verses)

CHORUS

Dance The Day Away

Words and Music by Don Mizell and Leonard Jones

Well, I've heard that in Jamaica
You can dance the day away
Bring all your friends and play

I've heard you can go dancing and prancing
You can just mambo and tango
You can dance the day away!

So come join us, everyone
Just laughing and having fun
There's so many ways to play
And dance the day away

You know that in our ocean
You can dance the day away
Bring all your friends and play

Well, you can go swimming
And spinning
You can go flipping and flapping
You can splash the day away

So come join us in the fun
We're laughing till day is done
There's so many ways to play
And dance the day away

This must be like Jamaica
We'll dance the day away
Bring all our friends and play

We will go dancing and prancing
We can go twisting and twirling
We can splash the day away

We can dance the day away
Bring all our friends and play
We can go dipping and diving
We can go dancing and prancing
We can dance the day away
We can dance the day away
Dance the day away

Dancing Mood

Words and Music by Alphonsus Cassell

Vibration so strong in the party
Electric eels dance all around me

Soca and calypso make me want to dance
Swinging to the tempo makes me want to dance

When the music thrills me, and the spirit grips me
No one can control me, the music enfolds me

I wanna dance, I wanna splash
I wanna splash, splash, splash!

CHORUS
I'm in a dancing mood, I'm in a dancing mood
I'm in a dancing mood, I'm in a dancing mood

I feel like dancing
Feel like prancing
Music jamming
Splashing, splashing!

CHORUS

Music is music, I'm a jammer
The kind of flavor doesn't matter

Salsa and the tango make me want to dance
Swinging to the tempo makes me want to dance

When the music thrills me, and the spirit grips me
No one can control me, the music enfolds me

I wanna dance, I wanna splash
I wanna splash, splash, splash!

CHORUS

I feel like dancing
Feel like prancing
Music jamming
Splashing, splashing!

CHORUS

Day-O

(The Banana Boat Song)
Words and Music by Irving Burgie and William Attaway

Day-o, day-o, daylight come shining on my home
Day! Me say day, me say day
Me say day, me say day, me say day-o
Daylight come shining on my home

Come, mister tally man, tally me banana
Come, mister tally man, tally me banana

A beautiful bunch of ripe banana
Daylight come shining on my home
Hide the deadly black tarantula

Day, me say day-o, daylight come shining
   on my home
Day! Me say day, me say day
Me say day, me say day, me say day, me say day-o

Come, mister tally man, tally me banana
Daylight come shining on my home
Come on, mister tally man, tally me banana
Daylight come shining on my home

Day-o, day-o, daylight come shining on my home
Day! Me say day-o, daylight come shining
   on my home

Six o'clock, seven o'clock, eight o'clock get up!
Daylight come shining on my home
And have some fruit juice and ripe banana
Daylight come shining on my home
Pineapple, mango, June plum and cassava
Daylight come shining on my home

Daylight come shining on my home
Daylight come shining on my home

Hot, Hot, Hot

Words and Music by Alphonsus Cassell

Olé olé olé olé
Olé olé olé olé

Me mind on fire
Me soul on fire
Feeling hot, hot, hot!

All the people all around me
Feeling hot, hot, hot!
A-what to do on a night like this?
Is it sweet?
I can't resist!
We need a party sound
A fundamental charm

CHORUS
So we can rhum-bum-bum-bum
Yeah rhum-bum-bum-bum
Feeling hot, hot, hot!
Feeling hot, hot, hot!

See people rocking
Hear people chanting
Feeling hot, hot, hot!
Keep up the spirit
Come on, let's hear it
Feeling hot, hot, hot!

It's in the air
Celebration time
Is it sweet?
Captivate your mind
We need this party sound
This fundamental charm

CHORUS

Feeling hot, hot, hot!
Feeling hot, hot, hot!

Olé olé olé olé
Olé olé olé olé
Olé olé olé olé
Olé olé olé olé
Feeling hot, hot, hot! (etc.)

Jamaica Farewell

Words and Music by Irving Burgie

Down the way where the nights are gay
And the moon shines gaily on the mountain top
I took a trip on a sailing ship
And when I reached Jamaica, I made a stop

CHORUS
But I'm sad to say, I'm on my way
Won't be back for many a day
My heart is down, my head is turning around
I had to leave a little crab in Kingston town

Sounds of laughter everywhere
And the dancing fish swaying to and fro
I must declare my heart is there
Though I've been from Maine to Mexico

CHORUS

Under the sea there
You can hear
Mer folk singing songs
That I love so dear
Fish are dancing everywhere
And the fun is fine any time of year.

CHORUS

Music Sweet

Words and Music by Winston Bailey

Prancing in a party, innocent and nice
When a man approached me to give an advice, yes
He told me I'm too small to be prancing so
I said, man, you're too tall, that's why you don't know

CHORUS
I don't want to behave bad
Oh, no (bad, bad!)
If this is behaving bad
Then how come I feeling so?
The music sweet – oh, yes
And I feeling the dance
The music sweet – yes, man
You don't want me to prance
Play the music, play the music
Play the music, play the music
Now, jam!
Sweet! Sweet! Sweet!
Play the music, play the music
Play the music, play the music

Tell me Mr. Noah, tell me when to dance
Maybe when I'm older and too weak to prance
When family business take control of me
And some bad arthritis inside of my knee

CHORUS (Repeat)

Take This Song

Words and Music by William Clarke, Michael Cooper, Stephen Coore, Richard Daley, Kenny Gamble, Claudine Nesbeth and William Stewart

Down in Jamaica
One Friday afternoon
A little bird brought us a song
With melody
He says, "Take this song
Give it to the whole, wide world
From now on, you're on your own
Remember that you're not alone"

Can't you see
That the whole world is changing?
Can't you see
There's a new day dawning?

I've come so far
So far from across the sea
I've traveled by day
Traveled by night
With a message to set you free

CHORUS
Take this song and melody
Make this world a symphony
Take this song and melody
Make this world a symphony

Can't you see
That the whole world is changing?
Can't you see
There's a new day dawning?

People sing
The same song around the world
A song of love
To touch the hearts
The hearts of everyone

CHORUS

He brought the message
Then he went away
He gave us hope for a brighter day
Gave us the strength
To make it through the storm
When seas are rough
Times are tough
It's up to us to carry on

CHORUS (Repeat)

Three Little Birds

Words and Music by Bob Marley

CHORUS
Don't worry about a thing
'Cause every little thing is gonna' be all right
Don't worry about a thing
'Cause every little thing is gonna' be all right

Rise up this morning
Smiled at the rising sun
Three little birds beside my doorstep
Singing sweet songs of melodies pure and true
Saying, "This is my message to you-oo-oo"
Singing...

CHORUS

(Repeat first verse)

CHORUS (Repeat)

Under The Sea

(From Walt Disney's "THE LITTLE MERMAID")
Words by Howard Ashman
Music by Alan Menken

The seaweed is always greener
In somebody else's lake
You dream about going up there
But that is a big mistake
Just look at the world around you
Right here on the ocean floor
Such wonderful things surround you
What more is you looking for?

Under the sea, under the sea
Darling it's better
Down where it's wetter
Take it from me
Up on the shore they work all day
Out in the sun they slave away
While we devoting
Full time to floating
Under the sea

Down here all the fish is happy
As off through the waves they roll
The fish on the land ain't happy
They sad 'cause they in the bowl
But fish in the bowl is lucky
They in for a worser fate
One day when the boss get hungry
Guess who gon' be on the plate?

Under the sea, under the sea
Nobody beat us fry us and eat us
In fricassee
We what the land folks loves to cook
Under the sea we off the hook
We got no troubles
Life is the bubbles

Under the sea, under the sea
Since life is sweet here
We got the beat here, naturally
Even the sturgeon and the ray
They get the urge and start to play
We got the spirit
You got to hear it
Under the sea

The newt play the flute
The carp play the harp
The plaice play the bass
And they sounding sharp
The bass play the brass
The chub play the tub
The fluke is the duke of soul

The ray he can play
The lings on the strings
The trout rockin' out
The blackfish she sings
The smelt and the sprat
They know where it's at
And oh, that blowfish blow!

Under the sea, under the sea
When the sardine begin the beguine
It's music to me
What do they got, a lot of sand?
We got a hot crustacean band!
Each little clam here
Know how to jam here
Under the sea

Each little slug here
Cutting a rug here
Under the sea
Each little snail here
Know how to wail here
That's why it's hotter
Under the water
Ya, we in luck here
Down in the muck here
Under the sea

You Can Get It If You Really Want

Words and Music by Jimmy Cliff

CHORUS
You can get it if you really want
You can get it if you really want
You can get it if you really want
But you must try, try and try, try and try
You'll succeed at last

Trying hard you must not fear
Win or lose you gonna' get your share
You've got your mind set on a dream
You can get it, tho' hard it may seem now

CHORUS

Rome was not built in a day
Opposition will come your way
But the harder the battle you see
Is the sweeter the victory!

CHORUS (Repeat)